VIRGINIA TEST PREP
Practice Test Book
SOL Mathematics
Grade 5

© 2018 by V. Hawas

All rights reserved. No part of this book may be reproduced or transmitted in any form or by any means, electronic, mechanical, photocopying, recording, or otherwise without prior written permission.

ISBN 978-1725634220

TEST MASTER PRESS

www.testmasterpress.com

CONTENTS

Introduction   **4**

SOL Mathematics: Mini-Tests   **5**
    Mini-Test 1   5
    Mini-Test 2   13

SOL Mathematics: Practice Test 1   **21**
    Section 1   21
    Section 2   31

SOL Mathematics: Practice Test 2   **42**
    Section 1   42
    Section 2   52

SOL Mathematics: Practice Test 3   **62**
    Section 1   62
    Section 2   73

SOL Mathematics: Practice Test 4   **83**
    Section 1   83
    Section 2   93

Answer Key   **105**
    Mini-Test 1   106
    Mini-Test 2   108
    Practice Test 1, Section 1   110
    Practice Test 1, Section 2   112
    Practice Test 2, Section 1   113
    Practice Test 2, Section 2   115
    Practice Test 3, Section 1   116
    Practice Test 3, Section 2   118
    Practice Test 4, Section 1   119
    Practice Test 4, Section 2   120

INTRODUCTION
For Parents, Teachers, and Tutors

About the SOL Mathematics Assessments

Students will be assessed each year by taking the SOL Mathematics assessments. This practice test book will prepare students for the assessments. It contains two mini-tests that will introduce students to the types of tasks they will need to complete. This is followed by four full-length practice tests similar to the real SOL Mathematics tests.

About the Standards of Learning

In 2016, the state of Virginia adopted new *Standards of Learning*. The *Standards of Learning* describe what students are expected to know. Student learning throughout the year is based on these standards, and all the questions on the SOL Mathematics assessments cover these standards. All the exercises and questions in this book cover the *Standards of Learning* introduced in 2016.

Types of Tasks on the SOL Mathematics Assessments

The SOL Mathematics tests are taken online as computer adaptive tests. These tests contain several question types, including technology-enhanced items. The questions types are described below.

- Multiple-choice – students select the one correct answer from four possible options.
- Fill-in-the-blank – students write a number or word in a blank space.
- Hot spot – students select one or more elements. These questions could involve selecting items, shading parts of a figure, completing a graph, or marking points on a number line.
- Drag and drop – students drag one or more draggers to drop zones. Draggers could be numbers, words, or symbols. These questions could involve writing fractions, completing an equation, placing numbers in order, or labeling items.

This practice test book contains multiple-choice questions and questions with similar formats to the technology-enhanced items. To ensure that students develop strong mathematics skills, this book also contains written answer questions. These questions will give students the opportunity to describe mathematics concepts and explain their thinking.

Taking the Tests

The first two mini-tests introduce students to the assessments with 10 questions that cover all the common question types. These short tests will allow students to become familiar with the types of questions they will encounter before moving on to longer tests. These shorter tests may also be used as guided instruction before allowing students to complete the assessments on their own.

The mini-tests are followed by four full-length practice tests. These have the same length, the same question types, and assess the same skills as the real SOL Mathematics tests. Just like the real SOL tests, the practice tests are divided into two sections. Students can complete the two sections on the same day or on different days, but should have a break between sessions.

SOL Mathematics

Grade 5

Mini-Test 1

Instructions

Read each question carefully. For each multiple-choice question, fill in the circle for the correct answer. For other types of questions, follow the directions given in the question.

You may use a ruler to help you answer questions. You may not use a calculator on this test.

1 Which word best describes the shape of the sign below?

- Ⓐ Scalene
- Ⓑ Equilateral
- Ⓒ Isosceles
- Ⓓ Right

2 The grid below represents the calculation of 0.4 × 0.2.

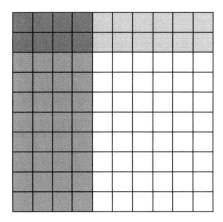

What is the value of 0.4 × 0.2? Write your answer below.

_____

3   Jonah filled the box below with 1-inch cubes. How many 1-inch cubes would it take to fill the box?

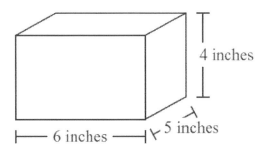

- Ⓐ   15
- Ⓑ   30
- Ⓒ   60
- Ⓓ   120

4   Which of these could be two of the angle measures of the right triangle below?

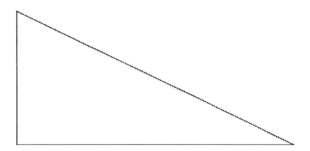

- Ⓐ   20° and 60°
- Ⓑ   25° and 65°
- Ⓒ   30° and 70°
- Ⓓ   45° and 75°

5 Place the sign <, >, or = in each empty box to correctly compare each pair of decimals.

0.06 ☐ 0.006

1.22 ☐ 1.42

5.669 ☐ 5.667

7.535 ☐ 7.505

0.85 ☐ 0.850

9.077 ☐ 9.770

6 Don spends $12.80 on four sandwiches. If each sandwich has the same cost, what is the cost of each sandwich? Write your answer below.

_____

7   Priya measures the lengths of pieces of timber, in inches. The lengths measured are listed below.

$$2\frac{1}{4}, 2\frac{3}{4}, 2\frac{1}{2}, 2\frac{1}{2}, 2\frac{1}{4}, 2, 2\frac{1}{4}, 2\frac{1}{2}, 2\frac{1}{4}, 2\frac{3}{4}$$

Use the data to complete the line plot below.

Pieces of Timber

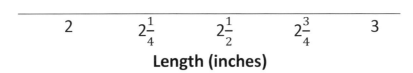

Length (inches)

Priya uses all the timber pieces with the most common length. What is the total length of the pieces Priya uses? Write your answer below.

_____ inches

8 A timber shelf has the measurements shown below.

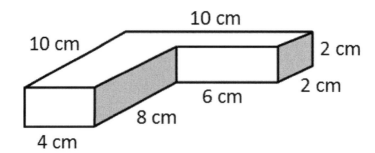

Determine **two** ways the shelf can be divided into two rectangular prisms. Write the dimensions of the **two** sets of rectangular prisms below.

Set 1 _____ by _____ by _____

and

_____ by _____ by _____

Set 2 _____ by _____ by _____

and

_____ by _____ by _____

What is the total volume of the timber shelf? Write your answer below. Be sure to include the correct units.

_____

10

9   Bradley has 64 1-inch cubic blocks. He uses all the blocks to build a rectangular prism that is 2 inches high and 2 inches wide. How long is the rectangular prism? Write your answer below.

_____ inches

Complete the table below to show the dimensions of **two** other rectangular prisms Bradley could make using all the blocks.

	Rectangular Prism 1	Rectangular Prism 2
Length		
Height		
Width		

Could Bradley use all the blocks to make a cube? Explain your answer.

_____

_____

_____

_____

10 Emma grouped the numbers from 10 to 20 into prime and composite numbers. Sort the numbers from 21 to 30 into prime and composite numbers. Write each number in the correct column of the table below.

Prime		Composite	
11	13	10	12
17	19	14	15
		16	18
		20	

Explain how the prime numbers are different from composite numbers.

_____

_____

_____

_____

END OF PRACTICE SET

SOL Mathematics

Grade 5

Mini-Test 2

Instructions

Read each question carefully. For each multiple-choice question, fill in the circle for the correct answer. For other types of questions, follow the directions given in the question.

You may use a ruler to help you answer questions. You may not use a calculator on this test.

1. Which number is a composite number?

- Ⓐ 63
- Ⓑ 67
- Ⓒ 89
- Ⓓ 97

2. The table shows the best times for running 100 meters of four students on the track team.

Student	Best Time (seconds)
Ramon	12.77
Ellis	12.63
Xavier	12.75
Colin	12.68

If each time is rounded to the nearest tenth, which student would have a best time of 12.7 seconds?

- Ⓐ Ramon
- Ⓑ Ellis
- Ⓒ Xavier
- Ⓓ Colin

3   Annabelle has 56 1-centimeter cubes. What are the dimensions of a rectangular prism Annabelle could build with all the cubes?

Ⓐ   7 units long, 4 units high, 2 units wide

Ⓑ   6 units long, 5 units high, 5 units wide

Ⓒ   10 units long, 2 units high, 3 units wide

Ⓓ   8 units long, 2 units high, 4 units wide

4   Circle the calculation that is represented on the grid below. Then find the value of the calculation. Write your answer on the line below.

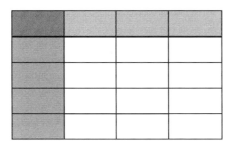

0.25 ÷ 0.2   0.25 ÷ 4   0.2 ÷ 4   0.2 ÷ 5

Answer _____

5 Select **all** the expressions below that are equal to $\frac{2}{3}$.

☐ $1 - \frac{1}{3}$

☐ $\frac{1}{6} + \frac{1}{6}$

☐ $\frac{1}{3} + \frac{1}{3}$

☐ $\frac{1}{6} + \frac{1}{6} + \frac{1}{6}$

☐ $3 - \frac{1}{3}$

☐ $\frac{5}{12} + \frac{3}{12}$

6 Bryant was reading a book with 220 pages. He read 90 pages in the first week. He wants to finish the book in 5 days. Write an expression that can be used to calculate how many pages he needs to read each day to finish the book in 5 days. Then simplify the expression to find the number of pages he needs to read each day.

Expression _____

Answer _____

7 A factory can fill 225 bottles of orange juice each hour. Each bottle of juice contains 24 fluid ounces of juice. Each bottle of juice sells for $5.50.

How many bottles of juice can be filled in each 12-hour shift? Write your answer below.

_____

If all the bottles made in a 12-hour shift sell, how much money will be made? Write your answer below.

_____

How many fluid ounces of juice are filled in each 12-hour shift? Write your answer below.

_____ fluid ounces

How many pints of juice are filled in each 12-hour shift? Write your answer below.

_____ pints

8   During a science experiment, Holly measured the lengths of ten acorns she collected. The lengths, in inches, are listed below.

$1\frac{1}{4}, 1\frac{5}{8}, 1\frac{1}{2}, 1\frac{1}{2}, 1\frac{1}{4}, 1\frac{1}{8}, 1\frac{1}{4}, 1\frac{1}{2}, 1\frac{1}{4}, 1\frac{3}{8}$

Use the data to complete the line plot below.

Acorns

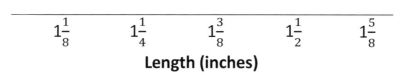

Length (inches)

What is the difference between the longest and the shortest acorn? Write your answer below.

_____ inches

9 In the space below, sketch and label a right angle, an acute angle, and an obtuse angle.

Right Angle

Acute Angle

Obtuse Angle

Which angle sketched had to be an exact angle measure? Explain your answer.

_____

_____

_____

_____

10 The stem-and-leaf plot shows the high temperature each day over a 3-week period for Greenville.

Daily High Temperature (°C)

Stem	Leaf
1	9 9
2	2 4 5 6 7 7 7 7 8 8 9 9 9
3	0 0 1 1 1 2

What was the highest temperature recorded? Write your answer on the line below.

_____ °C

END OF PRACTICE SET

SOL Mathematics

Grade 5

Practice Test 1

Section 1

Instructions

Read each question carefully. For each multiple-choice question, fill in the circle for the correct answer. For other types of questions, follow the directions given in the question.

You may use a ruler to help you answer questions. You may not use a calculator on this test.

1   The table below shows the ticket prices for a bus tour.

Ticket	Price
Adult	$5
Child	$3
Senior	$4

Sam's family paid exactly $15 for bus tickets. Which set of tickets could they have bought?

Ⓐ   1 adult, 2 child, and 1 senior

Ⓑ   2 adult, 1 child

Ⓒ   1 adult, 1 child, 2 senior

Ⓓ   3 child, 1 senior

2   What is the mean, median, and mode of the data below?

14, 14, 17, 15, 18, 20, 14

Draw a line to match each measure with its value.

mean   14

median   15

mode   16

3   A bakery sold 0.25 of its apple pies by lunch time. What fraction of the apple pies were sold by lunch time?

   Ⓐ $\frac{1}{25}$

   Ⓑ $\frac{1}{4}$

   Ⓒ $\frac{2}{5}$

   Ⓓ $\frac{3}{4}$

4   Lisa filled the box below with 1-centimeter cubes. How many 1-centimeter cubes would it take to fill the box?

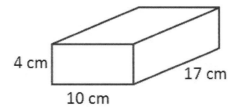

   Ⓐ 160

   Ⓑ 556

   Ⓒ 680

   Ⓓ 1,020

5   Gina states that the number 95 is a prime number. Which statement best explains how you can tell that Gina is incorrect?

Ⓐ   The number 95 can be evenly divided by 5.

Ⓑ   The number 95 is a two-digit number.

Ⓒ   The number 95 is an odd number.

Ⓓ   The number 95 is less than 100.

6   Erin is sorting 65 quarters into piles. She puts the quarters in piles of 5.

Complete the number sentence below to show how many piles of quarters Erin has.

_____ ÷ _____ = _____

7   Joanne had three singing lessons one week. Two lessons went for 45 minutes, and one lesson went for 60 minutes. Which number sentence could be used to find how many minutes Joanne had singing lessons for?

Ⓐ   (2 x 45) x 60

Ⓑ   (2 + 45) x 60

Ⓒ   (2 x 45) + 60

Ⓓ   (2 + 45) + 60

8   A school has 7 school buses. Each bus can seat 48 students. A total of 303 students get on the buses to go to a school camp. How many empty seats would there be on the buses? Write your answer below.

   _____

9   What is the value of the expression below? Write your answer below.

   $(16 + 20) - 8 \div 4$

   _____

10   Which situation would a stem-and-leaf plot best be used for?

   Ⓐ   How the number of students at a school has changed over the years

   Ⓑ   What fraction of people voted for each student in a school election

   Ⓒ   How the age and height of students is related

   Ⓓ   What score out of 100 thirty students got on a test

11 The stem-and-leaf plot shows the amount in tips Cleo earned on each day that she worked in July.

Tips Earned ($)

Stem	Leaf
2	2 4 8 9
3	0 0 2 3 5 5 5 7 7 8 9
4	0 1 1 4 8
5	2 5

On how many days did Cleo earn more than $50 in tips?

Ⓐ 2
Ⓑ 7
Ⓒ 25
Ⓓ 55

12 Mike went on vacation to Ohio. When he left home, the odometer read 7,219.4 miles. When he returned home, the odometer read 8,192.6 miles. How many miles did Mike travel? Write your answer below.

_____ miles

13   The table below shows the prices of items at a cake stall.

Item	Price
Small cake	$1.85
Muffin	$2.25
Cookie	$0.95

Frankie bought a small cake and a cookie. Bronwyn bought a muffin. How much more did Frankie spend than Bronwyn? Write your answer below.

_____

14   The 5 letter cards below are placed on a table. Baxter picks a letter card at random.

What is the probability that Baxter will pick a vowel?

Ⓐ   2 out of 3

Ⓑ   2 out of 5

Ⓒ   1 out of 2

Ⓓ   3 out of 5

15 Justine drew the triangle XYZ below.

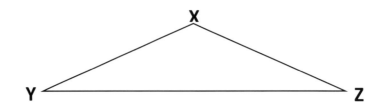

Based on the side lengths, what type of triangle is XYZ? Write your answer below.

_____

Explain why you classified the triangle that way.

_____

_____

_____

_____

_____

16 The table below shows the total cost of hiring DVDs for different numbers of DVDs.

Number of DVDs (d)	Total Cost, in Dollars (C)
2	6
5	15
6	18
8	24

Write an equation that describes the relationship between the number of DVDs hired, d, and the total cost in dollars, C. Write your equation below.

_____

17 Which of the following shapes can be divided into two congruent isosceles trapezoids?

Ⓐ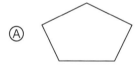

Ⓑ

Ⓒ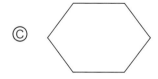

Ⓓ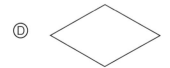

18. At the start of the week, a plant had a height of $\frac{5}{8}$ inches. The plant grew $\frac{1}{4}$ of an inch during the week. Which diagram is shaded to show the height of the plant at the end of the week?

Ⓐ

Ⓑ

Ⓒ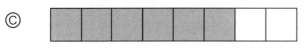

Ⓓ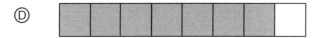

19. On May 1, Felipe paid $3.58 per gallon of fuel. On August 1, Felipe paid $3.71 per gallon of fuel. By how much did the price of fuel increase?

Ⓐ $0.03
Ⓑ $0.07
Ⓒ $0.13
Ⓓ $0.17

20. Which operation in the expression should be carried out first?

$$6 + 3 \times (8 - 2 \times 2)$$

Ⓐ 6 + 3
Ⓑ 3 × 8
Ⓒ 8 − 2
Ⓓ 2 × 2

END OF PRACTICE SET

SOL Mathematics

Grade 5

Practice Test 1

Section 2

Instructions

Read each question carefully. For each multiple-choice question, fill in the circle for the correct answer. For other types of questions, follow the directions given in the question.

You may use a ruler to help you answer questions. You may not use a calculator on this test.

1   Shade the diagrams below to show the subtraction. Then write the correct answer below on the blank line.

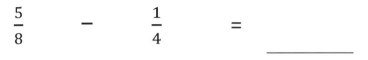

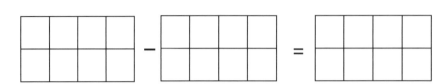

2   A 1-liter jug is filled with orange juice to the line shown.

Jacob pours 100 mL of orange juice into cups. How many cups could Jacob fill?

Ⓐ   2
Ⓑ   5
Ⓒ   10
Ⓓ   100

3   An orange tree has a height of 2.45 meters. What is the height of the tree in centimeters? Write your answer below.

_____ cm

4   Which diagram represents the sum of $\frac{1}{4}$ and $\frac{1}{8}$?

Ⓐ

Ⓑ

Ⓒ

Ⓓ

5   Which number is less than 35.052?

Ⓐ   35.009

Ⓑ   35.061

Ⓒ   35.101

Ⓓ   35.077

6   Which rectangles have a perimeter the same as the rectangle shown below? Select all the correct answers.

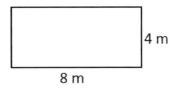

☐ 16 cm by 2 cm

☐ 7 cm by 5 cm

☐ 3 cm by 9 cm

☐ 10 cm by 3 cm

☐ 16 cm by 1 cm

☐ 14 cm by 6 cm

7   A pattern of numbers is shown below.

8, 13, 18, 23, 28, 33, 38, …

Circle **all** the numbers that could be numbers in the pattern.

41   53   60   65   67

71   76   88   92   99

8   An orchard has a total of 192 orange trees. They are planted in rows of 12 orange trees each. How many rows of orange trees does the orchard have? Write your answer below.

_____ rows

9   Joshua bought a pair of sunglasses for $14.85 and a phone case for $2.55. How much change should he receive from $20? Write your answer below.

$ _____

10 The model below was made with 1-inch cubes.

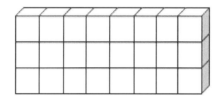

What is the volume of the model? Write your answer below. Be sure to include the correct units in your answer.

_____

11   Graham placed four candles against a ruler, as shown below.

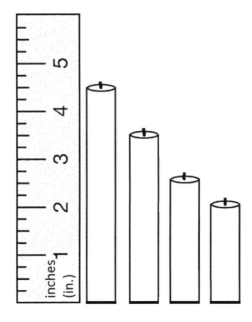

Find the heights of the four candles to the nearest half inch. Record the heights as decimals and list the heights from tallest to shortest.

Tallest   **Shortest**

_____ inches   _____ inches   _____ inches   _____ inches

12   Jordana grouped the numbers from 30 to 40 into prime and composite numbers.

Prime	Composite
31	30
37	32
	33
	34
	35
	36
	38
	39
	40

Which numbers from 41 to 50 should Jordana add to the list of prime numbers? Circle **all** the numbers that should be added.

41   42   43   44   45

46   47   48   49   50

13 What is the measure of the angle shown below?

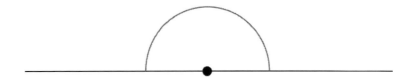

- Ⓐ 45°
- Ⓑ 90°
- Ⓒ 100°
- Ⓓ 180°

14 Shade the model below to show 1.4.

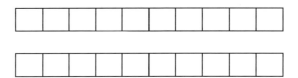

Use the model to find the value of 1.4 ÷ 2. Write your answer below.

_____

15 Which single transformation is represented in the models of the lightning bolts?

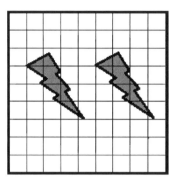

- Ⓐ Reflection
- Ⓑ Translation
- Ⓒ Rotation
- Ⓓ Dilation

16 Sandra started walking to school at 8:45 a.m. It took her 25 minutes to get to school. What time did she get to school?

- Ⓐ 9:00 a.m.
- Ⓑ 9:10 a.m.
- Ⓒ 9:15 a.m.
- Ⓓ 9:20 a.m.

17 It took James and his family $2\frac{1}{4}$ hours to drive from their house to the beach. How many minutes did the drive take? Write your answer below.

_____ minutes

18 Draw lines to match the correct term to the correct line on the diagram below.

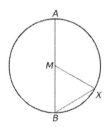

Line *AB*   radius

Line *MX*   chord

Line *BX*   diameter

19 Kevin is 1.45 meters tall. Brad is 20 centimeters taller than Kevin. What is Brad's height? Write your answer on the line.

_____ centimeters

20. Which pairs of numbers could be added to the table below? Select **all** the correct answers.

Number	Number ÷ 10
85.04	8.504
501.62	50.162
19.483	1.9483

☐ | 28.63 | 286.3 |

☐ | 3.65 | 0.365 |

☐ | 987.78 | 9.8778 |

☐ | 62.69 | 0.6269 |

☐ | 7.25 | 72.5 |

☐ | 46.77 | 4.677 |

END OF PRACTICE SET

SOL Mathematics

Grade 5

Practice Test 2

Section 1

Instructions

Read each question carefully. For each multiple-choice question, fill in the circle for the correct answer. For other types of questions, follow the directions given in the question.

You may use a ruler to help you answer questions. You may not use a calculator on this test.

1. To add the fractions below, Wayne first needs to determine the least common multiple of the denominators.

$$\frac{1}{5}, \frac{5}{7}, \frac{9}{10}$$

What is the least common multiple of the denominators? Write your answer below.

_____

2. The diagram below shows the length of a piece of ribbon.

0.12 meter

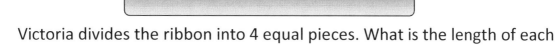

Victoria divides the ribbon into 4 equal pieces. What is the length of each piece of ribbon?

Ⓐ 0.3 meters

Ⓑ 0.4 meters

Ⓒ 0.03 meters

Ⓓ 0.04 meters

3 Donna has $8.45. She spends $3.75. How much money does Donna have left? Write your answer below.

$_____

4 Hannah cut out a piece of fabric to use for an art project. The length of the fabric was 9.5 yards. The width of the fabric was 3.6 yards less than the length. What was the width of the fabric?

  Ⓐ 5.9 yards

  Ⓑ 6.9 yards

  Ⓒ 12.1 yards

  Ⓓ 13.1 yards

5 Errol is putting photos into albums. Each album has 24 pages for holding photos, and each page can hold 8 photographs. How many photographs could Errol put into 3 photo albums?

  Ⓐ 192

  Ⓑ 376

  Ⓒ 486

  Ⓓ 576

6   Kathy answered $\frac{3}{5}$ of the questions on a test correctly. Which of the following is equivalent to $\frac{3}{5}$?

Ⓐ   0.3

Ⓑ   0.35

Ⓒ   0.6

Ⓓ   0.65

7   The graph below shows data a science class collected on the diameter of pebbles collected on a beach.

Pebble Diameter (inches)

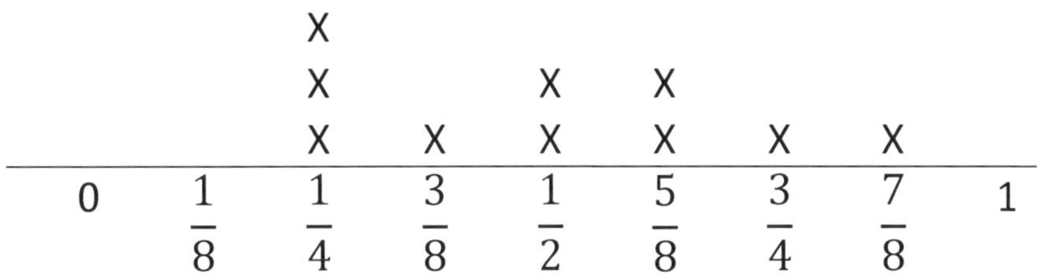

```
                X
                X               X       X
                X       X       X       X       X       X
    ─────────────────────────────────────────────────────────
        0      1/8     1/4     3/8     1/2     5/8     3/4     7/8     1
```

How many pebbles had diameters of $\frac{1}{2}$ inch or more?

Ⓐ   2

Ⓑ   4

Ⓒ   6

Ⓓ   10

8   To complete a calculation correctly, Mark moves the decimal place of 420.598 two places to the left.

$$420.598 \rightarrow 4.20598$$

Which of these describes the calculation completed?

- Ⓐ   Dividing by 10
- Ⓑ   Dividing by 100
- Ⓒ   Multiplying by 10
- Ⓓ   Multiplying by 100

9   Camille cooked a cake on high for $1\frac{1}{4}$ hours. She then cooked it for another $\frac{1}{2}$ hour on low. How long did she cook the cake for in all?

- Ⓐ $1\frac{1}{2}$ hours
- Ⓑ $1\frac{3}{4}$ hours
- Ⓒ $2\frac{1}{4}$ hours
- Ⓓ $2\frac{1}{2}$ hours

10 A play sold $224 worth of tickets. Each ticket cost the same amount. Which of these could be the cost of each ticket? Select **all** the possible answers.

☐ $6

☐ $8

☐ $12

☐ $14

☐ $16

☐ $18

11 A piece of note paper has side lengths of 12.5 centimeters. What is the area of the piece of note paper?

- Ⓐ 144.25 square centimeters
- Ⓑ 144.5 square centimeters
- Ⓒ 156.25 square centimeters
- Ⓓ 156.5 square centimeters

12 Liam drew a triangle with no equal side lengths, as shown below.

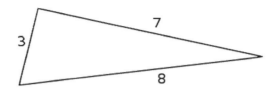

What type of triangle did Liam draw?

- Ⓐ Scalene
- Ⓑ Equilateral
- Ⓒ Isosceles
- Ⓓ Right

13 Sandy has $12.90. Marvin has $18.50. What is the total value of their money? Write your answer below.

$ _____

14 The top of a desk is 4 feet long and 3 feet wide. Raymond wants to cover the top of the desk with a vinyl sheet. The vinyl sheet is measured in square inches. What is the area of the vinyl sheet that will cover the top of the desk exactly?

- Ⓐ 12 square inches
- Ⓑ 144 square inches
- Ⓒ 168 square inches
- Ⓓ 1,728 square inches

15 Frankie swims laps of her pool each morning. It takes her 1.25 minutes to swim one lap. How long would it would take Frankie to swim 15 laps?

   Ⓐ 12.5 minutes

   Ⓑ 13.75 minutes

   Ⓒ 15.25 minutes

   Ⓓ 18.75 minutes

16 Denise made the line plot below to show how long she read for each weekday for 4 weeks.

Daily Reading Time (hours)

			X	
X			X	
X		X	X	
X		X	X	X
X	X	X	X	X
X	X	X	X	X
0	$\frac{1}{4}$	$\frac{1}{2}$	$\frac{3}{4}$	1

How long did Denise read for in total over the 4 weeks? Write your answer below.

_____ hours

17 The picture below shows the shirts and shorts that Damien has.

How many combinations of 1 shirt and 1 pair of shorts are possible?

Ⓐ 5

Ⓑ 6

Ⓒ 9

Ⓓ 8

18 The table below shows the total number of pounds of flour in different numbers of bags of flour.

Number of Bags	Number of Pounds
3	12
5	20
8	32
9	36

Based on the relationship in the table, how much flour is in each bag? Give your answer in pounds and then ounces. Write your answers below.

_____ pounds

_____ ounces

19 The model below is made up of 1-centimeter cubes. Complete the number sentence below to find the volume of the model.

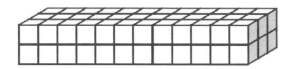

20 Which decimal is plotted on the number line below?

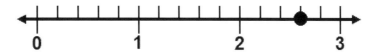

Ⓐ   2.25

Ⓑ   2.3

Ⓒ   2.6

Ⓓ   2.75

END OF PRACTICE SET

SOL Mathematics

Grade 5

Practice Test 2

Section 2

Instructions

Read each question carefully. For each multiple-choice question, fill in the circle for the correct answer. For other types of questions, follow the directions given in the question.

You may use a ruler to help you answer questions. You may not use a calculator on this test.

1   Brian made 16 paper cranes in 15 minutes. If he continues making cranes at this rate, how many cranes would he make in 2 hours? Write your answer below.

_____ paper cranes

2   The wingspan of the butterfly is 6.7 centimeters.

What is the wingspan of the butterfly in millimeters?

- Ⓐ 0.067 mm
- Ⓑ 0.67 mm
- Ⓒ 67 mm
- Ⓓ 670 mm

3   Jason used cubes to make the model shown below. What is the volume of the model?

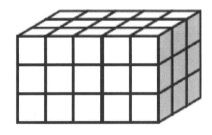

- Ⓐ   15 cubic units
- Ⓑ   45 cubic units
- Ⓒ   50 cubic units
- Ⓓ   75 cubic units

4   The pattern below starts at 0 and uses the rule "Add 4."

0, 4, 8, 12, 16

A second pattern starts at 2 and uses the rule "Add 4." How does the fifth term in the second pattern compare to the fifth term in the first pattern?

- Ⓐ   It is 2 greater.
- Ⓑ   It is 4 greater.
- Ⓒ   It is 8 greater.
- Ⓓ   It is 10 greater.

5   The table below shows how many customers a restaurant had on each day of the week.

Day	Number of Customers
Monday	28
Tuesday	21
Wednesday	36
Thursday	32
Friday	45

Which measure should be used to find the variation in the number of customers?

Ⓐ   Mean

Ⓑ   Median

Ⓒ   Mode

Ⓓ   Range

6   Which fractions can be placed in the empty box to make the statement below true? Select **all** the correct answers.

$$\frac{1}{4} < \boxed{}$$

☐ $\frac{5}{6}$ ☐ $\frac{3}{4}$ ☐ $\frac{1}{3}$ ☐ $\frac{1}{6}$

☐ $\frac{1}{2}$ ☐ $\frac{1}{8}$ ☐ $\frac{1}{10}$ ☐ $\frac{3}{12}$

7 Jason is buying baseball cards. Each packet of baseball cards contains 12 baseball cards and costs $3. How many baseball cards can Jason buy for $15? Write your answer below.

_____ baseball cards

8 Which pair of figures shows a reflection?

9. Corey wants to find the diameter of the penny below. Which of these would give Corey the diameter?

- Ⓐ Measure the distance from the edge to the center
- Ⓑ Measure the distance from one edge to the other, passing through the center
- Ⓒ Measure the distance around the edge
- Ⓓ Measure the distance from one point on the edge to any other point on the edge

10. The table shows the total cost of hiring different numbers of DVDs.

Number of DVDs	Total Cost, in Dollars
2	6
5	15
6	18
8	24

Which equation could be used to find the total cost in dollars, c, of hiring x DVDs?

- Ⓐ $c = x + 4$
- Ⓑ $c = 3x$
- Ⓒ $c = x + 3$
- Ⓓ $c = 8x$

11 Dave bought 4 packets of pies. Three packets had 12 pies each, and one packet had 10 pies. Which number sentence shows the total number of pies Dave bought?

- Ⓐ (3 x 12) x 10
- Ⓑ (3 + 12) x 10
- Ⓒ (3 x 12) + 10
- Ⓓ (3 + 12) + 10

12 Circle each number below that is a prime number.

5	7	13	18	23
37	46	51	62	73

13 The table below shows the cost of hiring items from a hire store.

Item	Cost per Week
CD	$2
DVD	$3
Video game	$4

Which expression represents the total cost, in dollars, of hiring c CDs and d DVDs for w weeks?

- Ⓐ $2c + 3d + w$
- Ⓑ $w(2c + 3d)$
- Ⓒ $w(2c) + 3d$
- Ⓓ $2c + 3d$

14 If the numbers below were each rounded to the nearest tenth, which **two** numbers would be rounded down? Select the **two** correct answers.

☐ 17.386

☐ 23.758

☐ 35.682

☐ 54.107

☐ 63.453

☐ 76.935

15 The model below was made with 1-unit cubes.

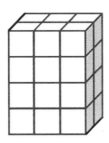

What is the volume of the model? Write your answer below.

_____ cubic units

16 The list below shows the height of 5 sunflowers in a garden.

Height (cm)
20
30
15
35
35

What is the median height of the sunflowers? Write your answer on the line below.

_____ cm

17 What is the value of $\frac{3}{10} + \frac{6}{10}$?

Ⓐ $\frac{9}{10}$

Ⓑ $\frac{9}{20}$

Ⓒ $\frac{9}{100}$

Ⓓ $\frac{18}{100}$

18 What is 9.627 rounded to the nearest hundredth?

Ⓐ 9.6

Ⓑ 9.7

Ⓒ 9.62

Ⓓ 9.63

19 The model below shows $1\frac{6}{100}$ shaded.

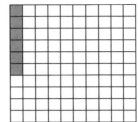

What decimal represents the shaded part of the model? Write your answer below.

_____

20 A rectangular toy box has a length of 90 centimeters, a width of 30 centimeters, and a height of 50 centimeters. What is the volume of the toy box?

  Ⓐ 4,500 cubic centimeters

  Ⓑ 6,000 cubic centimeters

  Ⓒ 81,000 cubic centimeters

  Ⓓ 135,000 cubic centimeters

END OF PRACTICE SET

SOL Mathematics

Grade 5

Practice Test 3

Section 1

Instructions

Read each question carefully. For each multiple-choice question, fill in the circle for the correct answer. For other types of questions, follow the directions given in the question.

You may use a ruler to help you answer questions. You may not use a calculator on this test.

1. A glass of water had a temperature of 25°C. Derek heated the water so that the temperature increased by 3°C every 10 minutes. What would the temperature of the water have been after 30 minutes?

    Ⓐ 28°C

    Ⓑ 31°C

    Ⓒ 34°C

    Ⓓ 37°C

2. Mr. Singh bought 2 adult zoo tickets for a total of $22, as well as 4 children's tickets. He spent $54 in total. How much was each children's ticket? Write your answer below.

    $ _____

3. Emily cooked a roast on high for $1\frac{1}{2}$ hours. She then cooked it for another $1\frac{3}{4}$ hour on low. How long did she cook the roast for in all?

    Ⓐ $2\frac{1}{4}$ hours

    Ⓑ $2\frac{3}{4}$ hours

    Ⓒ $3\frac{1}{4}$ hours

    Ⓓ $3\frac{3}{4}$ hours

4 Which operation in the expression should be carried out first?

$$42 + 24 \div (3 - 1) + 5$$

- Ⓐ 42 + 24
- Ⓑ 24 ÷ 3
- Ⓒ 3 − 1
- Ⓓ 3 + 5

5 Leanne added $\frac{1}{4}$ cup of milk and $\frac{3}{8}$ cup of water to a bowl. Shade the diagram below to show how many cups of milk and water were in the bowl in all.

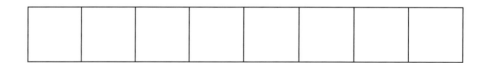

6 Taylor is making a stem-and-leaf plot to summarize the data below.

$$23, 26, 28, 36, 49$$

What numbers should be in the stem section of the plot?

- Ⓐ 2, 3, and 4
- Ⓑ 3, 6, 8, and 9
- Ⓒ 20, 30, and 40
- Ⓓ 23 and 49

7   The cost of renting a trailer is a basic fee of $20 plus an additional $25 for each day that the trailer is rented.

Which equation can be used to find c, the cost in dollars of the rental for d days?

Ⓐ   c = 20d + 25

Ⓑ   c = 25d + 20

Ⓒ   c = 20(d + 25)

Ⓓ   c = 25(d + 20)

8   Maxwell bought a packet of 48 baseball cards. He gave 8 baseball cards to each of 4 friends. Which number sentence can be used to find the number of baseball cards Maxwell has left?

Ⓐ   (48 − 8) × 4

Ⓑ   (48 − 8) ÷ 4

Ⓒ   48 − (8 + 4)

Ⓓ   48 − (8 × 4)

9   A square garden has side lengths of $4\frac{1}{2}$ feet. What is the area of the garden? You can use the diagram below to help find the answer.

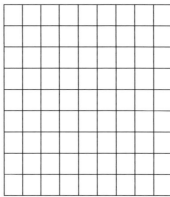

Each square is $\frac{1}{2}$ foot × $\frac{1}{2}$ foot.

Each square has an area of $\frac{1}{4}$ square feet.

Ⓐ $16\frac{1}{4}$ square feet

Ⓑ $20\frac{1}{4}$ square feet

Ⓒ $40\frac{1}{2}$ square feet

Ⓓ $182\frac{1}{4}$ square feet

10   Which fraction below is the greatest?

Ⓐ $\frac{7}{12}$

Ⓑ $\frac{1}{4}$

Ⓒ $\frac{2}{3}$

Ⓓ $\frac{5}{6}$

11 Courtney wants to make a garden with an area of 240 square feet. Select **all** the possible dimensions of the garden.

☐ 24 feet by 10 feet

☐ 40 feet by 80 feet

☐ 8 feet by 30 feet

☐ 6 feet by 20 feet

☐ 48 feet by 5 feet

☐ 100 feet by 20 feet

12 Which single transformation is represented below?

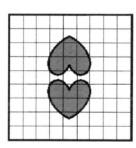

Ⓐ Reflection

Ⓑ Translation

Ⓒ Rotation

Ⓓ Dilation

13 Harris and Jamie both started with no savings. Harris saved $3 per week, while Jamie saved $6 per week.

Complete the table below to show Harris's and Jamie's total savings at the end of each week for the first 6 weeks.

Week	1	2	3	4	5	6
Harris's Total Savings						
Jamie's Total Savings						

Describe the relationship between Harris's total savings and Jamie's total savings each week.

_____

_____

_____

_____

14. The list below shows data a science class collected on the diameter of hailstones that fell during a storm.

Hailstone Diameter (inches)

$$\frac{1}{4}, \frac{1}{4}, \frac{1}{2}, \frac{5}{8}, \frac{1}{2}, \frac{3}{8}, \frac{5}{8}, \frac{1}{4}, \frac{7}{8}, \frac{3}{4}$$

Plot the data on the line plot below.

Hailstone Diameter (inches)

$0 \quad \frac{1}{8} \quad \frac{1}{4} \quad \frac{3}{8} \quad \frac{1}{2} \quad \frac{5}{8} \quad \frac{3}{4} \quad \frac{7}{8} \quad 1$

What is the difference in diameter between the largest hailstone and the smallest hailstone? Write your answer below.

_____ inches

15 Tom worked for 32 hours and earned $448. He earned the same rate per hour.

Write an equation that can be solved to find how much Tom earns per hour. Use *h* to represent how much Tom earns per hour.

Equation _____

Solve the equation to find how much Tom earns per hour. Write your answer below.

$ _____

16 Mitch ran 2.6 miles on Monday and 1.8 miles on Tuesday. How many miles less did Mitch run on Tuesday? Write your answer below. You can use the diagram below to find the answer.

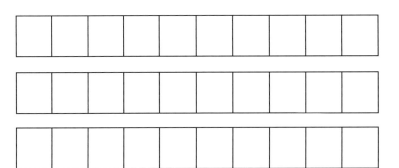

_____ miles

17 The model below is made up of 1-centimeter cubes. What is the volume of the model? Write your answer below.

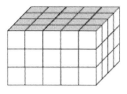

_____ cubic centimeters

18 Rory began studying one evening at the time shown on the clock below.

He studied for 1 hour and 20 minutes. What time did he finish studying?

Ⓐ   7:15 p.m.

Ⓑ   7:55 p.m.

Ⓒ   8:05 p.m.

Ⓓ   8:15 p.m.

19 Sushi sells for $3 for each small roll and $5 for each large roll.

Derrick bought 4 small rolls and 7 large rolls.

Complete the expression below to show how to find the total amount Derrick spent, in dollars.

(___ × ___) + (___ × ___)

Simplify the expression you wrote to find the total amount Derrick spent. Write your answer below.

$ _____

20 There are 10 new students at Kerry's elementary school. Of those students, $\frac{2}{5}$ are female students. How many new female students are there? Write your answer below.

_____ students

END OF PRACTICE SET

SOL Mathematics

Grade 5

Practice Test 3

Section 2

Instructions

Read each question carefully. For each multiple-choice question, fill in the circle for the correct answer. For other types of questions, follow the directions given in the question.

You may use a ruler to help you answer questions. You may not use a calculator on this test.

1   The decimal cards for 0.59 and 0.22 are shown below.

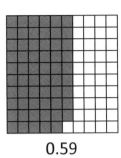
0.59

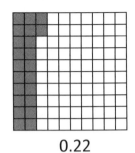
0.22

What is the difference of 0.59 and 0.22? Write your answer below.

_____

2   Look at the fractions below.

$$1\tfrac{1}{3},\ 2\tfrac{1}{2},\ 3\tfrac{5}{6}$$

Which procedure can be used to find the sum of the fractions?

Ⓐ   Find the sum of the whole numbers, find the sum of the fractions, and then add the two sums

Ⓑ   Find the sum of the whole numbers, find the sum of the fractions, and then multiply the two sums

Ⓒ   Find the sum of the whole numbers, find the sum of the fractions, and then subtract the two sums

Ⓓ   Find the sum of the whole numbers, find the sum of the fractions, and then divide the two sums

3 Joy made 24 apple pies for a bake sale. Each serving was $\frac{1}{8}$ of a pie. How many servings did Joy make?

Ⓐ 3
Ⓑ 32
Ⓒ 96
Ⓓ 192

4 Which of these shapes can be divided into two equal triangles by drawing a vertical line down the center?

Ⓐ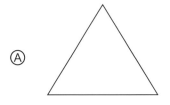

Ⓑ

Ⓒ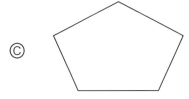

Ⓓ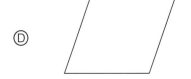

5   A diner has 18 tables. Each table can seat 4 people. The diner also has 8 benches that can each seat 6 people. How many people can the diner seat in all?

Ⓐ 36
Ⓑ 120
Ⓒ 260
Ⓓ 308

6   The stem-and-leaf plot shows Becky's score on ten weekly quizzes.

Student Ages

Stem	Leaf
0	9 9
1	2 3 3 3 6 6 8 9

What was Becky's most common score?

Ⓐ 3
Ⓑ 9
Ⓒ 13
Ⓓ 19

7   What is the value of the expression below? Write your answer below.

$$42 + 24 \div 3 + 3$$

_____

8   The number set below represents the number of questions that eight students answered correctly on a test.

42, 67, 87, 65, 67, 73, 86, 84

Which measure of data is represented by the number 67?

Ⓐ   Mode

Ⓑ   Median

Ⓒ   Mean

Ⓓ   Range

9 Chan spent $\frac{3}{8}$ of his total homework time completing his science homework. What calculation could be used to convert the fraction to a decimal?

   Ⓐ $3 \div 8 \times 100$

   Ⓑ $8 \div 3 \times 100$

   Ⓒ $3 \div 8$

   Ⓓ $8 \div 3$

10 A recipe for pancakes requires $2\frac{2}{3}$ cups of flour. Donna only has $1\frac{1}{2}$ cups of flour. How many more cups of flour does Donna need?

   Ⓐ $\frac{1}{3}$ cup

   Ⓑ $\frac{1}{6}$ cup

   Ⓒ $1\frac{1}{3}$ cups

   Ⓓ $1\frac{1}{6}$ cups

11 There are 6 reams of paper in a box. There are 144 boxes of paper on a pallet. How many reams of paper are on a pallet? Write your answer below.

   _____

12. Byron made 9 baskets out of 15 baskets he attempted. What fraction of his baskets did he make? Write the fraction below and then simplify it to lowest terms.

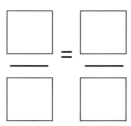

13. The angle that is formed between two lines has a measure of 95°. Which term describes this angle?

   Ⓐ Acute

   Ⓑ Right

   Ⓒ Obtuse

   Ⓓ Straight

14. The table below shows a set of number pairs.

x	y
1	1
3	5
5	9

   Which equation shows the relationship between x and y?

   Ⓐ y = x + 2

   Ⓑ y = x + 4

   Ⓒ y = 2x – 1

   Ⓓ y = 3x – 4

15 Leonard is ordering a milkshake. He can choose chocolate or vanilla in either small, medium, or large. Complete the list to represent all the different combinations of flavor and size he could choose.

CS   CM   _____

_____   _____   _____

16 The table below shows how long Chelsea spent doing yoga during the week.

Day	Time (minutes)
Monday	20
Tuesday	30
Wednesday	15
Thursday	35
Friday	35

What is the mean of the amount of time Chelsea spent doing yoga each day?

Ⓐ   20 minutes

Ⓑ   27 minutes

Ⓒ   30 minutes

Ⓓ   35 minutes

17 The circumference of a basketball is 75.8 cm.

What is the circumference of the basketball in millimeters? Write your answer on the line below.

_____ millimeters

18 The table below shows the relationship between the original price and the sale price of a book.

Original price, P	Sale price, S
$10	$7.50
$12	$9
$14	$10.50
$16	$12

What is the rule to find the sale price of a book, in dollars? Add the missing number to the rule below.

S = _____ P

19 Leo measures the length, width, and height of a block. He multiplies the length, width, and height. What is Leo finding?

- Ⓐ Surface area
- Ⓑ Mass
- Ⓒ Volume
- Ⓓ Perimeter

20 Circle **all** the figures below that have at least one right angle.

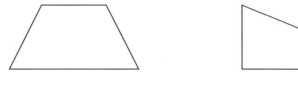

END OF PRACTICE SET

SOL Mathematics

Grade 5

Practice Test 4

Section 1

Instructions

Read each question carefully. For each multiple-choice question, fill in the circle for the correct answer. For other types of questions, follow the directions given in the question.

You may use a ruler to help you answer questions. You may not use a calculator on this test.

---

1. The cost of renting a windsurfer is a basic fee of $15 plus an additional $5 for each hour that the windsurfer is rented. Which equation can be used to find c, the cost in dollars of the rental for h hours?

   Ⓐ $c = 15h + 5$

   Ⓑ $c = 5h + 15$

   Ⓒ $c = 15(h + 5)$

   Ⓓ $c = 5(h + 15)$

2. Look at the group of numbers below.

108	86	282
164	190	76

   What do these numbers have in common?

   Ⓐ They are all even numbers.

   Ⓑ They are all odd numbers.

   Ⓒ They are all greater than 100.

   Ⓓ They are all less than 200.

3   What decimal is equivalent to the fraction $\frac{33}{100}$?

   Ⓐ   0.033

   Ⓑ   0.33

   Ⓒ   33.0

   Ⓓ   3.3

4   A recipe for a cake requires $1\frac{2}{3}$ cups of flour. Fill in the blank box below to show $1\frac{2}{3}$ as an improper fraction.

5   Which single transformation is shown below?

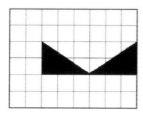

   Ⓐ   Translation

   Ⓑ   Reflection

   Ⓒ   Rotation

   Ⓓ   Dilation

6   The two containers below are the same size and are filled with different amounts of water.

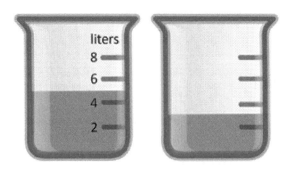

Georgie pours all the water from the first container into the second. How much water would be in the second container in all?

Ⓐ   5 liters

Ⓑ   7 liters

Ⓒ   8 liters

Ⓓ   9 liters

7   The table below shows the total number of lemons in different numbers of bags of lemons.

Number of Bags (B)	Number of Lemons (L)
2	16
3	24
5	40
8	64

What is the relationship between the total number of lemons, L, and the number of bags of lemons, B? Complete the equation below to show the relationship.

L = ____B

8   Amy ordered 3 pizzas for $6.95 each. She also bought a soft drink for $1.95. Which equation can be used to find how much change, c, she should receive from $30?

Ⓐ   c = 30 – 3(6.95 + 1.95)

Ⓑ   c = 30 – 3(6.95 – 1.95)

Ⓒ   c = 30 – 6.95 – 1.95

Ⓓ   c = 30 – (6.95 × 3) – 1.95

9   What is the decimal 55.146 rounded to the nearest whole number, nearest tenth, and nearest hundredth? Write your answers below.

Nearest whole number _____

Nearest tenth _____

Nearest hundredth _____

10   What is the value of the expression below? Write your answer below.

$$28 + 4 \div 2 + (9 - 5)$$

_____

11. The table shows the side length of a rhombus and the perimeter of a rhombus.

Side Length, x (cm)	Perimeter, y (cm)
1	4
2	8
3	12
4	16

Which equation represents the relationship between side length and perimeter?

Ⓐ $y = x + 3$

Ⓑ $y = 4x$

Ⓒ $x = y + 4$

Ⓓ $x = 4y$

12. A florist sells balloons in sets of 6. A customer ordered several sets of 6 balloons. Which of these could be the total number of balloons ordered? Circle **all** the correct possible answers.

48   50   54   58   62

66   70   78   80   88

13 The table shows the amount of Don's phone bill for four different months.

Month	Amount
April	$12.22
May	$12.09
June	$12.18
July	$12.05

Place the months in order from the lowest bill to the highest bill. Write the months on the lines below.

Lowest   _____

_____

_____

Highest   _____

14 Marcus sold drinks at a lemonade stand. The table shows how many drinks of each size he sold.

Size	Number Sold
Small	15
Medium	20
Large	5
Extra large	10

Which size drink made up $\frac{3}{10}$ of the total sold? Write your answer below.

_____

15   What is the rule to find the value of a term in the sequence below?

Position, n	Value of Term
1	3
2	5
3	7
4	9

Ⓐ   4n – 4

Ⓑ   3n

Ⓒ   2n + 1

Ⓓ   n + 2

16   The table shows the amount of rainfall for the first five days of May.

Date	1st	2nd	3rd	4th	5th
Rainfall (cm)	4.59	4.18	4.50	4.61	4.73

Compare the five decimals. Write the decimals on the lines below.

_____ < _____ < _____ < _____ < _____

17 What value of x makes the equation below true? Write your answer below.

$$54 \div x = 9$$

x = _____

18 The grid below represents 4 x 7.

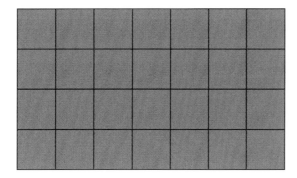

Which of these is another way to represent 4 x 7? Select **all** the correct answers.

☐ 7 × 4

☐ 7 + 7 + 7 + 7

☐ 7 + 7 + 7 + 7 + 7 + 7 + 7

☐ 4 + 4 + 4 + 4

☐ 4 x 4 x 4 x 4

☐ 4 + 4 + 4 + 4 + 4 + 4 + 4

19 Sandy has 129 dimes. Marvin has 185 dimes. What is the total value of Sandy and Marvin's dimes?

- Ⓐ $3.04
- Ⓑ $3.14
- Ⓒ $30.40
- Ⓓ $31.40

20 The diagram below shows the dimensions of a school's stage.

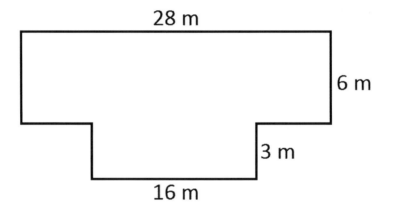

What is the perimeter of the stage? Write your answer on the line below.

_____ meters

END OF PRACTICE SET

SOL Mathematics

Grade 5

Practice Test 4

Section 2

Instructions

Read each question carefully. For each multiple-choice question, fill in the circle for the correct answer. For other types of questions, follow the directions given in the question.

You may use a ruler to help you answer questions. You may not use a calculator on this test.

1   Ellen multiplies the number 3 by a fraction. The result is a number greater than 3. Which of these could be the fraction?

Ⓐ $1\frac{1}{4}$

Ⓑ $\frac{8}{9}$

Ⓒ $\frac{1}{6}$

Ⓓ $\frac{1}{2}$

2   Mrs. Morgan is choosing the design of a business card. The picture below shows the patterns and the colors available.

Plain	Pink	Green
Stars	Blue	Red
Stripes	Yellow	Silver

If Mrs. Morgan chooses a pattern and a color at random, what is the probability she gets a pink business card with stars on it?

Ⓐ   1 out of 9

Ⓑ   1 out of 12

Ⓒ   1 out of 18

Ⓓ   1 out of 36

3   Lloyd bought 4 T-shirts. Each T-shirt cost $7. Which is one way to work out how much change Lloyd would receive from $30?

- Ⓐ Add 4 to 7 and subtract the result from 30
- Ⓑ Add 4 to 7 and add the result to 30
- Ⓒ Multiply 4 by 7 and add the result to 30
- Ⓓ Multiply 4 by 7 and subtract the result from 30

4   An Italian restaurant sells four types of meals. The owner made this table to show how many meals of each type were sold one night. According to the table, which statements are true? Select **all** the correct statements.

Meal	Number Sold
Pasta	16
Pizza	18
Salad	11
Risotto	9

- ☐ The store sold more pizza meals than salad and risotto meals combined.
- ☐ The store sold twice as many pizza meals as risotto meals.
- ☐ The store sold more pasta meals than any other type of meal.
- ☐ The store sold half as many salad meals as pasta meals.
- ☐ The store sold over 50 meals in total.

5   Jordan is putting CDs in a case. She can fit 24 CDs in each row. She has 120 CDs. Which equation can be used to find the total number of rows, r, she can fill?

Ⓐ   r × 120 = 24

Ⓑ   r ÷ 24 = 120

Ⓒ   120 × 24 = r

Ⓓ   120 ÷ 24 = r

6   Jay made 8 trays of 6 muffins each.

He gave 12 muffins away. He packed the remaining muffins in bags of 4 muffins each. Which expression can be used to find how many bags of muffins he packed?

Ⓐ   (8 × 6) − 12 ÷ 4

Ⓑ   (8 × 6) − (12 ÷ 4)

Ⓒ   8 × (6 − 12 ÷ 4)

Ⓓ   (8 × 6 − 12) ÷ 4

7 The table shows the side length of an equilateral triangle and the perimeter of an equilateral triangle.

Side Length, *l* (inches)	Perimeter, *P* (inches)
2	6
3	9
4	12
5	15

Which equation represents the relationship between side length and perimeter?

Ⓐ $P = l + 4$

Ⓑ $P = 3l$

Ⓒ $l = P + 4$

Ⓓ $l = 3P$

8 Which term describes the triangle below?

Ⓐ Isosceles

Ⓑ Scalene

Ⓒ Equilateral

Ⓓ Right

9   The stem-and-leaf plot shows the ages of students in an art class.

Student Ages

Stem	Leaf
1	7 9
2	2 2 4 6 6 6 8 9
3	0 1 1 1 2 7 7
4	1 5 6

Which expression shows how to find how much older the oldest student is than the youngest student?

Ⓐ   41 – 19 = 22

Ⓑ   41 – 17 = 24

Ⓒ   46 – 19 = 27

Ⓓ   46 – 17 = 29

10   Which statement is true about the product of $\frac{1}{3}$ and 6?

Ⓐ   The product is greater than 6.

Ⓑ   The product is less than $\frac{1}{3}$.

Ⓒ   The product is a value between the two factors.

Ⓓ   The product is a value equal to one of the factors.

11   Place the numbers listed below in order from lowest to highest.

   35.061   35.101   35.077   35.009

   Lowest   _____

              _____

              _____

   Highest   _____

12   A rectangular cutting board is 16 inches long and 11 inches wide. What is the perimeter of the cutting board?

   Ⓐ   27 inches
   Ⓑ   54 inches
   Ⓒ   108 inches
   Ⓓ   176 inches

13 The table below shows how many customer complaints a business had each year since 2000.

Year	Number of Complaints
2000	28
2001	21
2002	36
2003	32
2004	45
2005	92
2006	89
2007	76
2008	48
2009	43
2010	56
2011	32
2012	30

Which measure should be used to find the variation in the number of complaints each year?

Ⓐ   Mean

Ⓑ   Median

Ⓒ   Mode

Ⓓ   Range

14 A right triangle is shown below.

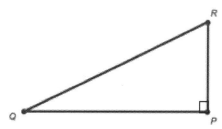

If angle Q measures 35°, what is the measure of angle R? Write your answer below.

_____°

15 Look at the triangles below.

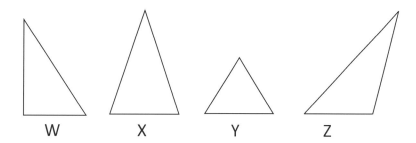

Connor classifies triangles X and Y as isosceles triangles because they have a pair of equal sides. What error has Connor made?

Ⓐ   He has not recognized that triangle Y has more than 2 equal sides.

Ⓑ   He has not considered the angle measures of triangle X.

Ⓒ   He has not recognized that triangle X only has 2 equal sides.

Ⓓ   He has not considered whether triangles X and Y have right angles.

16 A restaurant manager kept a record of the pieces of pie sold one week. He made this list to show the results.

- $\frac{1}{4}$ of the pieces sold were apple pie
- $\frac{3}{8}$ of the pieces sold were pumpkin pie
- $\frac{1}{12}$ of the pieces sold were cherry pie
- The rest of the pieces sold were peach pie.

What fraction of the pieces sold were peach pie? Write your answer below.

_____

17 Karen made this table to show the amount she spent on lunch each day one week.

Day	Amount
Monday	$5.73
Tuesday	$5.49
Wednesday	$5.51
Thursday	$5.27
Friday	$5.80

What is the total amount Karen spent on lunch that week? Write your answer below.

$ _____

18 Plot the number 3.8 on the number line below.

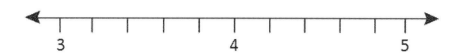

What is 3.8 rounded to the nearest whole number? Write your answer below.

_____

On the lines below, explain how the number line helped you round the number.

_____

_____

_____

19 Circle the measurements that are equivalent to 600 centimeters.

    0.6 mm   6 mm   60 mm   6000 mm

    0.6 m   6 m   60 m   6000 m

Convert 600 centimeters to kilometers. Write your answer below.

_____ kilometers

20 The model below is made up of 1-centimeter cubes.

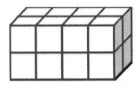

Write and solve an equation to find the volume of the model.

Volume: _____ cubic centimeters

If the height of the model is doubled, how does the volume of the model change? Explain your answer.

_____

_____

_____

_____

END OF PRACTICE SET

ANSWER KEY

Virginia's New State Standards

In 2016, the state of Virginia adopted new *Standards of Learning*. The *Standards of Learning* describe what students are expected to know. Student learning throughout the year is based on these standards, and all the questions on the SOL Mathematics assessments cover these standards. All the exercises and questions in this book cover the *Standards of Learning* introduced in 2016.

Assessing Skills and Knowledge

The skills listed in the *Standards of Learning* are divided into five topics. These are:

- Number and Number Sense
- Computation and Estimation
- Measurement and Geometry
- Probability and Statistics
- Patterns, Functions, and Algebra

The answer key identifies the topic for each question. Use the topics listed to identify general areas of strength and weakness. Then target revision and instruction accordingly.

The answer key also identifies the specific math skill that each question is testing. Use the skills listed to identify skills that the student is lacking. Then target revision and instruction accordingly.

Scoring Questions

This book includes questions where a task needs to be completed or a written answer is provided. The answer key gives guidance on what to look for in the answer and how to score these questions. Use the criteria listed as a guide to scoring these questions, and as a guide for giving the student advice on how to improve an answer.

SOL Mathematics, Mini-Test 1

Question	Answer	Topic	Mathematics Standard
1	B	Measurement and Geometry	Classify triangles as right, acute, or obtuse and equilateral, scalene, or isosceles.
2	0.08	Computation and Estimation	Estimate and determine the product and quotient of two numbers involving decimals.
3	D	Measurement and Geometry	Solve practical problems that involve perimeter, area, and volume in standard units of measure.
4	B	Measurement and Geometry	Investigate the sum of the interior angles in a triangle and determine an unknown angle measure.
5	>, <, >, >, =, <	Number and Number Sense	Compare and order fractions, mixed numbers, and/or decimals in a given set, from least to greatest and greatest to least.
6	$3.20	Computation and Estimation	Create and solve single-step and multistep practical problems involving addition, subtraction, and multiplication of decimals, and create and solve single-step practical problems involving division of decimals.
7	See Below	Probability and Statistics	Represent data in line plots and stem-and-leaf plots. Interpret data represented in line plots and stem-and-leaf plots.
8	See Below	Measurement and Geometry	Solve practical problems that involve perimeter, area, and volume in standard units of measure.
9	See Below	Measurement and Geometry	Solve practical problems that involve perimeter, area, and volume in standard units of measure.
10	See Below	Number and Number Sense	Identify and describe the characteristics of prime and composite numbers.

Q7.
The line plot should be completed as shown below.

Pieces of Timber

	X			
	X	X		
	X	X	X	
X	X	X	X	
2	$2\frac{1}{4}$	$2\frac{1}{2}$	$2\frac{3}{4}$	3

Length (inches)

Answer: 9 inches

Scoring Information
Give a total score out of 3.
Give a score out of 2 for the line plot.
Give a score of 1 for the correct answer.

Q8.
The following two sets of dimensions should be listed. (Measurements can be listed in any order.)
10 cm by 2 cm by 2 cm and 4 cm by 8 cm by 2 cm
4 cm by 10 cm by 2 cm and 6 cm by 2 cm by 2 cm

Answer: 104 cubic centimeters or 104 cm³

Scoring Information
Give a total score out of 3.
Give a score of 1 for each set of correct dimensions.
Give a score of 1 for the correct answer.

Q9.
16 inches
Each column in the table should be completed with any combination of length, height, and width that multiply to 64. Possible answers include: 4, 8, and 2; 64, 1, and 1; 8, 8, and 1; or 32, 2, and 1.

The student should identify that Bradley could make a cube. The explanation should describe how the cube would have side lengths of 4 and a volume of 64 cubic inches. The explanation may include the calculation 4 × 4 × 4 = 64.

Scoring Information
Give a total score out of 6.
Give a score of 1 for a correct answer of 16 inches.
Give a score of 1 for each column of the table completed correctly.
Give a score of 1 for identifying that Bradley could make a cube.
Give a score out of 2 for the explanation.

Q10.
Prime: 23, 29
Composite: 21, 22, 24, 25, 26, 27, 28, 30
The student should explain that prime numbers can only be divided by themselves and 1, while composite numbers can be divided by at least one other number.

Scoring Information
Give a total score out of 4.
Give a score out of 2 for sorting the numbers correctly.
Give a score out of 2 for the explanation.

SOL Mathematics, Mini-Test 2

Question	Answer	Topic	Mathematics Standard
1	A	Number and Number Sense	Identify and describe the characteristics of prime and composite numbers.
2	D	Number and Number Sense	Given a decimal through thousandths, round to the nearest whole number, tenth, or hundredth.
3	A	Measurement and Geometry	Solve practical problems that involve perimeter, area, and volume in standard units of measure.
4	0.2 ÷ 4 0.05	Computation and Estimation	Estimate and determine the product and quotient of two numbers involving decimals.
5	1st, 3rd, and 6th	Computation and Estimation	Solve single-step and multistep practical problems involving addition and subtraction with fractions and mixed numbers.
6	(220 − 90) ÷ 5 26	Computation and Estimation	Create and solve single-step and multistep practical problems involving addition, subtraction, multiplication, and division of whole numbers.
7	See Below	Computation and Estimation	Create and solve single-step and multistep practical problems involving addition, subtraction, and multiplication of decimals, and create and solve single-step practical problems involving division of decimals.
8	See Below	Probability and Statistics	Represent data in line plots and stem-and-leaf plots. Interpret data represented in line plots and stem-and-leaf plots.
9	See Below	Measurement and Geometry	Classify and measure right, acute, obtuse, and straight angles.
10	32°C	Probability and Statistics	Interpret data represented in line plots and stem-and-leaf plots.

Q7.
2,700
$14,850
64,800 fluid ounces
4,050 pints

Scoring Information
Give a total score out of 4.
Give a score of 1 for each correct answer.

Q8.
The line plot should be completed as shown below.

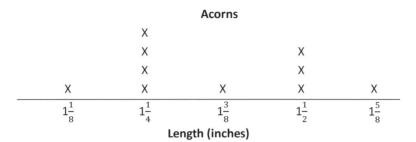

Answer: $\frac{1}{2}$ inches

Scoring Information
Give a total score out of 3.
Give a score out of 2 for the line plot.
Give a score of 1 for the correct answer.

Q9.
The student should sketch a right angle equal to 90°, an acute angle of less than 90°, and an obtuse angle greater than 90°. The explanation should show an understanding that the right angle must be 90°, while the other two angles do not have to be an exact measure.

Scoring Information
Give a total score out of 4.
Give a score of 0.5 for each angle correctly sketched.
Give a score of 0.5 for identifying that the right angle had to be exact.
Give a score out of 2 for the explanation.

SOL Mathematics, Practice Test 1, Section 1

Question	Answer	Topic	Mathematics Standard
1	A	Computation and Estimation	Create and solve single-step and multistep practical problems involving addition, subtraction, multiplication, and division of whole numbers.
2	mean, 16 median, 15 mode, 14	Probability and Statistics	Determine the mean, median, mode, and range of a set of data.
3	B	Number and Number Sense	Represent and identify equivalencies among fractions and decimals, with and without models.
4	C	Measurement and Geometry	Solve practical problems that involve perimeter, area, and volume in standard units of measure.
5	A	Number and Number Sense	Identify and describe the characteristics of prime and composite numbers.
6	$65 \div 5 = 13$	Computation and Estimation	Create and solve single-step and multistep practical problems involving addition, subtraction, multiplication, and division of whole numbers.
7	C	Computation and Estimation	Create and solve single-step and multistep practical problems involving addition, subtraction, multiplication, and division of whole numbers.
8	33	Computation and Estimation	Create and solve single-step and multistep practical problems involving addition, subtraction, multiplication, and division of whole numbers.
9	34	Computation and Estimation	Simplify whole number numerical expressions using the order of operations.
10	D	Probability and Statistics	Represent data in line plots and stem-and-leaf plots.
11	A	Probability and Statistics	Interpret data represented in line plots and stem-and-leaf plots.
12	973.2 miles	Computation and Estimation	Create and solve single-step and multistep practical problems involving addition, subtraction, and multiplication of decimals, and create and solve single-step practical problems involving division of decimals.
13	$0.55 or 55 cents	Computation and Estimation	Create and solve single-step and multistep practical problems involving addition, subtraction, and multiplication of decimals, and create and solve single-step practical problems involving division of decimals.
14	B	Probability and Statistics	Determine the probability of an outcome by constructing a sample space or using the Fundamental (Basic) Counting Principle.
15	See Below	Measurement and Geometry	Classify triangles as right, acute, or obtuse and equilateral, scalene, or isosceles.
16	$C = 3d$	Patterns, Functions, and Algebra	Write an equation to represent a given mathematical relationship, using a variable.
17	C	Measurement and Geometry	Investigate and describe the results of combining and subdividing polygons.
18	D	Computation and Estimation	Solve single-step and multistep practical problems involving addition and subtraction with fractions and mixed numbers.
19	C	Computation and Estimation	Create and solve single-step and multistep practical problems involving addition, subtraction, and multiplication of decimals, and create and solve single-step practical problems involving division of decimals.
20	D	Computation and Estimation	Simplify whole number numerical expressions using the order of operations.

Q15.
isosceles

The student should explain that the triangle has two sides of equal length and one side of a different length.

Scoring Information
Give a total score out of 3.
Give a score of 1 for the correct answer.
Give a score out of 2 for the explanation.

SOL Mathematics, Practice Test 1, Section 2

Question	Answer	Topic	Mathematics Standard
1	$\dfrac{3}{8}$	Computation and Estimation	Solve single-step and multistep practical problems involving addition and subtraction with fractions and mixed numbers.
2	B	Measurement and Geometry	Solve practical problems involving length, mass, and liquid volume using metric units.
3	245 cm	Measurement and Geometry	Given the equivalent measure of one unit, identify equivalent measurements within the metric system.
4	B	Computation and Estimation	Solve single-step and multistep practical problems involving addition and subtraction with fractions and mixed numbers.
5	A	Number and Number Sense	Compare and order fractions, mixed numbers, and/or decimals in a given set, from least to greatest and greatest to least.
6	2nd and 3rd	Measurement and Geometry	Solve practical problems that involve perimeter, area, and volume in standard units of measure.
7	53, 88	Patterns, Functions, and Algebra	Identify, describe, create, express, and extend number patterns found in objects, pictures, numbers and tables.
8	16 rows	Computation and Estimation	Create and solve single-step and multistep practical problems involving addition, subtraction, multiplication, and division of whole numbers.
9	$2.60	Computation and Estimation	Create and solve single-step and multistep practical problems involving addition, subtraction, and multiplication of decimals, and create and solve single-step practical problems involving division of decimals.
10	24 cubic inches	Measurement and Geometry	Solve practical problems that involve perimeter, area, and volume in standard units of measure.
11	4.5, 3.5, 2.5, 2.0	Measurement and Geometry	Solve practical problems involving length, mass, and liquid volume using metric units.
12	41, 43, 47	Number and Number Sense	Identify and describe the characteristics of prime and composite numbers.
13	D	Measurement and Geometry	Classify and measure right, acute, obtuse, and straight angles.
14	0.7	Computation and Estimation	Estimate and determine the product and quotient of two numbers involving decimals.
15	B	Measurement and Geometry	Recognize and apply transformations, such as translation, reflection, and rotation.
16	C	Measurement and Geometry	Solve practical problems related to elapsed time in hours and minutes within a 24-hour period.
17	135 minutes	Measurement and Geometry	Solve practical problems related to elapsed time in hours and minutes within a 24-hour period.
18	Line *AB*, diameter Line *MX*, radius Line *BX*, chord	Measurement and Geometry	Identify and describe the diameter, radius, chord, and circumference of a circle.
19	165 cm	Measurement and Geometry	Solve practical problems involving length, mass, and liquid volume using metric units.
20	3.65, 0.365, 46.77, 4.677	Computation and Estimation	Create and solve single-step and multistep practical problems involving addition, subtraction, and multiplication of decimals, and create and solve single-step practical problems involving division of decimals.

SOL Mathematics, Practice Test 2, Section 1

Question	Answer	Topic	Mathematics Standard
1	70	Computation and Estimation	Solve single-step and multistep practical problems involving addition and subtraction with fractions and mixed numbers.
2	C	Computation and Estimation	Create and solve single-step and multistep practical problems involving addition, subtraction, and multiplication of decimals, and create and solve single-step practical problems involving division of decimals.
3	$4.70	Computation and Estimation	Create and solve single-step and multistep practical problems involving addition, subtraction, and multiplication of decimals, and create and solve single-step practical problems involving division of decimals.
4	A	Computation and Estimation	Create and solve single-step and multistep practical problems involving addition, subtraction, and multiplication of decimals, and create and solve single-step practical problems involving division of decimals.
5	D	Computation and Estimation	Create and solve single-step and multistep practical problems involving addition, subtraction, multiplication, and division of whole numbers.
6	C	Number and Number Sense	Represent and identify equivalencies among fractions and decimals, with and without models.
7	C	Probability and Statistics	Interpret data represented in line plots and stem-and-leaf plots.
8	B	Computation and Estimation	Create and solve single-step and multistep practical problems involving addition, subtraction, and multiplication of decimals, and create and solve single-step practical problems involving division of decimals.
9	B	Computation and Estimation	Solve single-step and multistep practical problems involving addition and subtraction with fractions and mixed numbers.
10	$8, $14, $16	Computation and Estimation	Create and solve single-step and multistep practical problems involving addition, subtraction, multiplication, and division of
11	C	Measurement and Geometry	Solve practical problems that involve perimeter, area, and volume in standard units of measure.
12	A	Measurement and Geometry	Classify triangles as right, acute, or obtuse and equilateral, scalene, or isosceles.
13	$31.40	Computation and Estimation	Create and solve single-step and multistep practical problems involving addition, subtraction, and multiplication of decimals, and create and solve single-step practical problems involving division of decimals.
14	D	Measurement and Geometry	Solve practical problems that involve perimeter, area, and volume in standard units of measure.
15	D	Measurement and Geometry	Estimate and determine the product and quotient of two numbers involving decimals.
16	10 hours	Probability and Statistics	Interpret data represented in line plots and stem-and-leaf plots.
17	B	Probability and Statistics	Determine the probability of an outcome by constructing a sample space or using the Fundamental (Basic) Counting Principle.

18	4 pounds 64 ounces	Patterns, Functions, and Algebra	Identify, describe, create, express, and extend number patterns found in objects, pictures, numbers and tables.
19	2 × 3 × 12 = 72 cm³	Measurement and Geometry	Solve practical problems that involve perimeter, area, and volume in standard units of measure.
20	C	Number and Number Sense	Represent and identify equivalencies among fractions and decimals, with and without models.

SOL Mathematics, Practice Test 2, Section 2

Question	Answer	Topic	Mathematics Standard
1	128	Measurement and Geometry	Solve practical problems related to elapsed time in hours and minutes within a 24-hour period.
2	C	Measurement and Geometry	Given the equivalent measure of one unit, identify equivalent measurements within the metric system.
3	B	Measurement and Geometry	Solve practical problems that involve perimeter, area, and volume in standard units of measure.
4	A	Patterns, Functions, and Algebra	Identify, describe, create, express, and extend number patterns found in objects, pictures, numbers and tables.
5	D	Probability and Statistics	Describe the range of a set of data as a measure of spread.
6	$\frac{5}{6}, \frac{3}{4}, \frac{1}{2}, \frac{1}{3}$	Number and Number Sense	Compare and order fractions, mixed numbers, and/or decimals in a given set, from least to greatest and greatest to least.
7	60 baseball cards	Number and Number Sense	Create and solve single-step and multistep practical problems involving addition, subtraction, multiplication, and division of whole numbers.
8	C	Measurement and Geometry	Recognize and apply transformations, such as translation, reflection, and rotation.
9	B	Measurement and Geometry	Identify and describe the diameter, radius, chord, and circumference of a circle.
10	B	Patterns, Functions, and Algebra	Write an equation to represent a given mathematical relationship, using a variable.
11	C	Computation and Estimation	Create and solve single-step and multistep practical problems involving addition, subtraction, multiplication, and division of whole numbers.
12	5, 7, 13, 23, 37, 73	Number and Number Sense	Identify and describe the characteristics of prime and composite numbers.
13	B	Patterns, Functions, and Algebra	Write an equation to represent a given mathematical relationship, using a variable.
14	35.682 63.543	Number and Number Sense	Given a decimal through thousandths, round to the nearest whole number, tenth, or hundredth.
15	24 cubic units	Measurement and Geometry	Solve practical problems that involve perimeter, area, and volume in standard units of measure.
16	30 cm	Probability and Statistics	Determine the mean, median, mode, and range of a set of data.
17	A	Computation and Estimation	Solve single-step and multistep practical problems involving addition and subtraction with fractions and mixed numbers.
18	D	Number and Number Sense	Given a decimal through thousandths, round to the nearest whole number, tenth, or hundredth.
19	1.06	Number and Number Sense	Represent and identify equivalencies among fractions and decimals, with and without models.
20	D	Measurement and Geometry	Solve practical problems that involve perimeter, area, and volume in standard units of measure.

SOL Mathematics, Practice Test 3, Section 1

Question	Answer	Topic	Mathematics Standard
1	C	Patterns, Functions, and Algebra	Identify, describe, create, express, and extend number patterns found in objects, pictures, numbers and tables.
2	$8	Computation and Estimation	Create and solve single-step and multistep practical problems involving addition, subtraction, multiplication, and division of whole numbers.
3	C	Computation and Estimation	Solve single-step and multistep practical problems involving addition and subtraction with fractions and mixed numbers.
4	C	Computation and Estimation	Simplify whole number numerical expressions using the order of operations.
5	5 of the 8 squares shaded	Computation and Estimation	Solve single-step and multistep practical problems involving addition and subtraction with fractions and mixed numbers.
6	A	Probability and Statistics	Represent data in line plots and stem-and-leaf plots.
7	B	Patterns, Functions, and Algebra	Write an equation to represent a given mathematical relationship, using a variable.
8	D	Computation and Estimation	Create and solve single-step and multistep practical problems involving addition, subtraction, multiplication, and division of whole numbers.
9	B	Measurement and Geometry	Solve practical problems that involve perimeter, area, and volume in standard units of measure.
10	D	Number and Number Sense	Compare and order fractions, mixed numbers, and/or decimals in a given set, from least to greatest and greatest to least.
11	1st, 3rd, 5th	Measurement and Geometry	Solve practical problems that involve perimeter, area, and volume in standard units of measure.
12	A	Measurement and Geometry	Recognize and apply transformations, such as translation, reflection, and rotation.
13	See Below	Patterns, Functions, and Algebra	Identify, describe, create, express, and extend number patterns found in objects, pictures, numbers and tables.
14	See Below	Probability and Statistics	Represent data in line plots and stem-and-leaf plots. Interpret data represented in line plots and stem-and-leaf plots.
15	$448 = 32h$ $14	Patterns, Functions, and Algebra	Use an expression with a variable to represent a given verbal expression involving one operation.
16	0.8 miles	Computation and Estimation	Create and solve single-step and multistep practical problems involving addition, subtraction, and multiplication of decimals, and create and solve single-step practical problems involving division of decimals.
17	60 cubic centimeters	Measurement and Geometry	Solve practical problems that involve perimeter, area, and volume in standard units of measure.
18	D	Measurement and Geometry	Solve practical problems related to elapsed time in hours and minutes within a 24-hour period.
19	(4 × 3) + (7 × 5) $47	Computation and Estimation	Create and solve single-step and multistep practical problems involving addition, subtraction, multiplication, and division of whole numbers.
20	4 students	Computation and Estimation	Solve single-step practical problems involving multiplication of a whole number, limited to 12 or less, and a proper fraction, with models.

Q13.
The student should complete the table with the following values:

Harris's Total Savings	3	6	9	12	15	18
Jamie's Total Savings	6	12	18	24	30	36

The student should explain that Jamie's total savings are always twice Harris's total savings.

Scoring Information
Give a total score out of 4.
Give a score of 1 for the correct values for Harris's Total Savings.
Give a score of 1 for the correct values for Jamie's Total Savings.
Give a score out of 2 for the explanation.

Q14.
The work should show the completed graph as below.

Hailstone Diameter (inches)

```
                X
                X               X       X
                X       X       X       X       X       X
  |_____|_____|_____|_____|_____|_____|_____|_____
  0    1/8     1/4     3/8     1/2     5/8     3/4     7/8    1
```

Answer: $\frac{5}{8}$ inches

Scoring Information
Give a total score out of 3.
Give a score out of 2 for the line plot.
Give a score of 1 for the correct answer.

SOL Mathematics, Practice Test 3, Section 2

Question	Answer	Topic	Mathematics Standard
1	0.37	Computation and Estimation	Create and solve single-step and multistep practical problems involving addition, subtraction, and multiplication of decimals, and create and solve single-step practical problems involving division of decimals.
2	A	Computation and Estimation	Solve single-step and multistep practical problems involving addition and subtraction with fractions and mixed numbers.
3	D	Computation and Estimation	Create and solve single-step and multistep practical problems involving addition, subtraction, multiplication, and division of whole numbers.
4	A	Measurement and Geometry	Investigate and describe the results of combining and subdividing polygons.
5	B	Computation and Estimation	Create and solve single-step and multistep practical problems involving addition, subtraction, multiplication, and division of whole numbers.
6	C	Probability and Statistics	Interpret data represented in line plots and stem-and-leaf plots.
7	53	Computation and Estimation	Simplify whole number numerical expressions using the order of operations.
8	A	Probability and Statistics	Determine the mean, median, mode, and range of a set of data.
9	C	Number and Number Sense	Represent and identify equivalencies among fractions and decimals, with and without models.
10	D	Computation and Estimation	Solve single-step and multistep practical problems involving addition and subtraction with fractions and mixed numbers.
11	864	Computation and Estimation	Create and solve single-step and multistep practical problems involving addition, subtraction, multiplication, and division of whole numbers.
12	9/15 = 3/5	Number and Number Sense	Represent and identify equivalencies among fractions and decimals, with and without models.
13	C	Measurement and Geometry	Classify and measure right, acute, obtuse, and straight angles.
14	C	Patterns, Functions, and Algebra	Write an equation to represent a given mathematical relationship, using a variable.
15	CL, VS, VM, VL	Probability and Statistics	Determine the probability of an outcome by constructing a sample space or using the Fundamental (Basic) Counting Principle.
16	B	Probability and Statistics	Determine the mean, median, mode, and range of a set of data.
17	758 mm	Measurement and Geometry	Given the equivalent measure of one unit, identify equivalent measurements within the metric system.
18	$S = 0.75p$ OR $S = \frac{3}{4}p$	Patterns, Functions, and Algebra	Write an equation to represent a given mathematical relationship, using a variable.
19	C	Measurement and Geometry	Differentiate among perimeter, area, and volume.
20	triangle rectangle	Measurement and Geometry	Classify and measure right, acute, obtuse, and straight angles.

SOL Mathematics, Practice Test 4, Section 1

Question	Answer	Topic	Mathematics Standard
1	B	Patterns, Functions, and Algebra	Write an equation to represent a given mathematical relationship, using a variable.
2	A	Number and Number Sense	Identify and describe the characteristics of even and odd numbers.
3	B	Number and Number Sense	Represent and identify equivalencies among fractions and decimals, with and without models.
4	5	Number and Number Sense	Represent and identify equivalencies among fractions and decimals, with and without models.
5	B	Measurement and Geometry	Recognize and apply transformations, such as translation, reflection, and rotation.
6	C	Measurement and Geometry	Solve practical problems involving length, mass, and liquid volume using metric units.
7	$L = 8B$	Patterns, Functions, and Algebra	Write an equation to represent a given mathematical relationship, using a variable.
8	D	Patterns, Functions, and Algebra	Write an equation to represent a given mathematical relationship, using a variable.
9	55 55.1 55.15	Number and Number Sense	Given a decimal through thousandths, round to the nearest whole number, tenth, or hundredth.
10	34	Computation and Estimation	Simplify whole number numerical expressions using the order of operations.
11	B	Patterns, Functions, and Algebra	Identify, describe, create, express, and extend number patterns found in objects, pictures, numbers and tables.
12	48 54 66 78	Computation and Estimation	Create and solve single-step and multistep practical problems involving addition, subtraction, multiplication, and division of whole numbers.
13	July May June April	Number and Number Sense	Compare and order fractions, mixed numbers, and/or decimals in a given set, from least to greatest and greatest to least.
14	Small	Number and Number Sense	Represent and identify equivalencies among fractions and decimals, with and without models.
15	C	Patterns, Functions, and Algebra	Identify, describe, create, express, and extend number patterns found in objects, pictures, numbers and tables.
16	4.18 < 4.50 < 4.59 < 4.61 < 4.73	Number and Number Sense	Compare and order fractions, mixed numbers, and/or decimals in a given set, from least to greatest and greatest to least.
17	6	Computation and Estimation	Create and solve single-step and multistep practical problems involving addition, subtraction, multiplication, and division of whole numbers.
18	1st, 2nd, and 6th	Computation and Estimation	Create and solve single-step and multistep practical problems involving addition, subtraction, multiplication, and division of whole numbers.
19	D	Computation and Estimation	Create and solve single-step and multistep practical problems involving addition, subtraction, and multiplication of decimals, and create and solve single-step practical problems involving division of decimals.
20	74 meters	Measurement and Geometry	Solve practical problems that involve perimeter, area, and volume in standard units of measure.

SOL Mathematics, Practice Test 4, Section 2

Question	Answer	Topic	Mathematics Standard
1	A	Computation and Estimation	Solve single-step practical problems involving multiplication of a whole number, limited to 12 or less, and a proper fraction, with models.
2	C	Probability and Statistics	Determine the probability of an outcome by constructing a sample space or using the Fundamental (Basic) Counting Principle.
3	D	Computation and Estimation	Create and solve single-step and multistep practical problems involving addition, subtraction, multiplication, and division of whole numbers.
4	2nd and 5th	Computation and Estimation	Create and solve single-step and multistep practical problems involving addition, subtraction, multiplication, and division of whole numbers.
5	D	Patterns, Functions, and Algebra	Write an equation to represent a given mathematical relationship, using a variable.
6	D	Computation and Estimation	Create and solve single-step and multistep practical problems involving addition, subtraction, multiplication, and division of whole numbers.
7	B	Patterns, Functions, and Algebra	Identify, describe, create, express, and extend number patterns found in objects, pictures, numbers and tables.
8	A	Measurement and Geometry	Classify triangles as right, acute, or obtuse and equilateral, scalene, or isosceles.
9	D	Probability and Statistics	Interpret data represented in line plots and stem-and-leaf plots.
10	C	Computation and Estimation	Solve single-step practical problems involving multiplication of a whole number, limited to 12 or less, and a proper fraction, with models.
11	35.009, 35.061, 35.077, 35.101	Number and Number Sense	Compare and order fractions, mixed numbers, and/or decimals in a given set, from least to greatest and greatest to least.
12	B	Measurement and Geometry	Solve practical problems that involve perimeter, area, and volume in standard units of measure.
13	D	Probability and Statistics	Describe the range of a set of data as a measure of spread.
14	55°	Measurement and Geometry	Investigate the sum of the interior angles in a triangle and determine an unknown angle measure.
15	A	Measurement and Geometry	Classify triangles as right, acute, or obtuse and equilateral, scalene, or isosceles.
16	$\frac{7}{24}$	Computation and Estimation	Solve single-step and multistep practical problems involving addition and subtraction with fractions and mixed numbers.
17	$27.80	Computation and Estimation	Create and solve single-step and multistep practical problems involving addition, subtraction, and multiplication of decimals, and create and solve single-step practical problems involving division of decimals.
18	See Below	Number and Number Sense	Given a decimal through thousandths, round to the nearest whole number, tenth, or hundredth.
19	6000 mm, 6 m, 0.006 kilometers	Measurement and Geometry	Given the equivalent measure of one unit, identify equivalent measurements within the metric system.
20	See Below	Measurement and Geometry	Solve practical problems that involve perimeter, area, and volume in standard units of measure.

Q18.
The number 3.8 should be plotted on the number line.
Answer: 4
The student should explain how you can tell that the number is closer to 4 than 3.

Scoring Information
Give a total score out of 3.
Give a score of 1 for the number correctly plotted.
Give a score of 1 for the correct answer.
Give a score out of 1 for the explanation.

Q20.
The student should write and solve the equation 2 × 2 × 4 = 16.
Volume: 16 cubic centimeters

The student should identify that the volume would double if the height doubled. The student could explain that doubling one of the values in the calculation doubles the result. The student could also double the height and show that 4 × 2 × 4 = 32, which is double 16.

Scoring Information
Give a total score out of 4.
Give a score of 1 for a correct equation.
Give a score of 1 for the correct volume.
Give a score out of 2 for the explanation.

Get to Know Our Product Range

Mathematics

Practice Test Books
Practice sets and practice tests will prepare students for the state tests.

Quiz Books
Focused individual quizzes cover every math skill one by one.

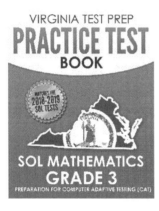  

Reading

Practice Test Books
Practice sets and practice tests will prepare students for the state tests.

Reading Skills Workbooks
Short passages and question sets will develop and improve reading comprehension skills.

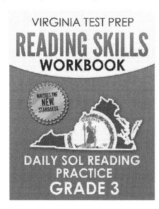  

Writing

Writing Skills Workbooks
Students write narratives, essays, and opinion pieces, and write in response to passages.

Persuasive and Narrative Writing Workbooks
Guided workbooks teach all the skills required to write effective narratives and opinion pieces.

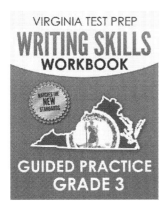  

Language

Language Quiz Books
Focused quizzes cover spelling, grammar, writing conventions, and vocabulary.

Revising and Editing Workbooks
Students improve language and writing skills by identifying and correcting errors.

Language Skills Workbooks
Exercises on specific language skills including idioms, synonyms, and homophones.

 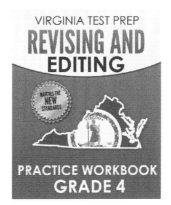 

http://www.testmasterpress.com

Made in United States
Orlando, FL
25 August 2024

50735295R00070